John H. Van Evrie

Subgenation:

The theory of the normal relation of the races

John H. Van Evrie

Subgenation:
The theory of the normal relation of the races

ISBN/EAN: 9783337884963

Printed in Europe, USA, Canada, Australia, Japan

Cover: Foto ©ninafisch / pixelio.de

More available books at **www.hansebooks.com**

SUBGENATION:

THE THEORY OF

The Normal Relation of the Races;

AN ANSWER TO

"MISCEGENATION."

"I thank thee, Jew, for teaching me that word."—SHAKSPEARE.

INTRODUCTORY.

Scaliger quaintly observes "that nothing will sell better than a scurrile pamphlet," and the extensive sale of a recent brochure, entitled "Miscegenation," in which the most indecent doctrines are seductively inculcated under the garb of philosophy, seems to prove the assertion. While there is no excuse for the gross violation of natural instincts which that author recommends, yet there is probably some good reason why there is a want of a popular knowledge as to the true relation of the races. The juxtaposition of the Caucasian, Indian, and Negro races on this continent, in considerable numbers, has no parallel in history. If we except the Egyptians and the Carthagenians, there were no ancient nations which had other than a homogeneous population. A negro was a curiosity in Greece and Rome. All modern Europe, from which we derive our language, is composed of one race or the varieties of it. The question, as to the proper relation of *distinct* races, is, therefore, a new one, and has been committed to this country for solution.

The writer to whom allusion has been made offers a solution, and it is no less a proposition than the annihilation of all the existing races and the formation of a new one! He proposes to bring this about by mingling the races, and has invented the word Miscegenation to express his idea (*miscere*, to mix; *genus*, a race). The suggestion of the word is a good one. The necessity of new terms to express the proper, as well as the improper, relation of the races on this continent has long been felt by thoughtful minds. The words slavery and slave are derived from *Sclavi—Sclavonians*, who were conquered by the Germans and reduced to abject bondage. The word, therefore, expresses a relation existing between persons of the *same* race, and not between those of *different* races. Hence it is a misnomer as applied to the American form of society. The present writer proposes to profit by the suggestion of the author of "Miscegenation," and coin another word, long needed. It is sub-

GENATION, from *sub*, lower, and *generatus* and *genus*, a race born or created lower than another; *i. e.*, the natural or normal relation of an inferior to a superior race. The invention of new words has the high authority of Horace:

> "Si forte necesse est
> Indiciis monstrare recentribus abdita rerum."

They were never so much needed as now. The simple truth is—*There is no slavery in this country; there are no slaves in the Southern States.* We are fighting about a myth. For three centuries the Christian world was deluged in blood upon the assumption that there was a Holy Sepulchre at Jerusalem. There was no Holy Sepulchre there. The world was fighting on a false premise. This country is now repeating the same insensate folly. In the following pages the writer proposes to show how and why this is so, to expose the errors and absurdities of the author of "Miscegenation," and to give such a solution to the question of the proper relation of the races as shall commend itself to the conscience of every intelligent friend of Humanity.

NEW WORDS USED IN THIS BOOK.

Subgenation—from the Latin *Sub*, lower, and *Generatus* and *Genus*, a race born or created lower than another; hence, the natural or normal relation of an inferior race.

Subgen—is used to describe the persons of the inferior races thus placed in their natural positions. Plural form, *Subgens.*

I.

THE DIVERSITY OF THE RACES.

"The teachings of physiology as well as the inspirations of Christianity, settle the question that all the tribes which inhabit the earth were originally derived from one type," says the author of "Miscegenation." This is a bold assertion, unsupported by proof, and yet it is this premise, thus audaciously assumed, which is the foundation of his whole argument. Demolish this and every thing else that he says, disappears "as the baseless fabric of a vision." Now the writer of this pamphlet undertakes to assert, and he will proceed to prove, that "the teachings of physiology and the inspirations of Christianity," warrant no such a conclusion, but on the contrary, lead to exactly the opposite opinion. The writer of "Miscegenation," would impress the public with the idea that no respectable authority questions his assumption, and yet the illustrious Agassiz has declared that "the view of mankind, as originating from a single pair, Adam and Eve, is neither a Biblical view nor a correct view, nor one agreeing with the results of science; and profound veneration for the Sacred Scriptures prompts us to pronounce *the prevailing view of the origin of man*, animals and plants, as a mere human hypothesis, not entitled to more consideration than belongs to most theories formed in the infancy of science."

The theory, however, that there is but a single human race, and that all man-*kind*, of whatever color, or mental or moral powers, are derived from it, is the very foundation and starting point of the entire Abolition and Miscegenetic doctrines. It will be well to notice it, therefore, with some degree of minuteness, for it is this ideal "brotherhood" of man which transports otherwise sensible men and women from the solid plain of facts and common sense into the realms of fiction and absurdity.

> "No Centaurs here nor Gorgons look to find,
> *My* subject is of man and human kind."

One of the great obstacles in the way of light and truth upon the important subject of the question of races, has been the absurd and narrow interpretation given to the Bible by commentators and ecclesiastics generally. If a history of the attempts of theologians to restrict or suppress the progress of science were fully written, it would be one of the most interesting and instructive works of the day. In the earlier middle ages a monk named Cosmas, represented the earth as a parallelogrammical plain, indented by the inland seas—the Mediterranean, the Caspian, the Red Sea, and the Persian Gulf—and encompassed by a rectangular trench occupied by the oceans! A copy of the "Geography of Cosmas," is now preserved in the British Museum, and a curious and amusing document it is. A drawing of it resembles an aquarium. A council of clergymen met in Salamanca, in 1486, to hear the views of Christopher Columbus. But a considerable portion held it to be grossly heterodox to believe that by sailing westward the eastern portion of the world could be reached! The idea that the world was round, not flat, was denounced by such renowned theologians as Lactantius and St. Augustine. "They observed," says Irving, in his "Life of Columbus," "that in the Psalms the heavens are said to be extended like a hide—that is, according to commentators, the curtain or covering of a tent, which among the ancient pastoral nations was formed of the hides of animals." The facts of geography, however, finally triumphed over the theories of ecclesiastics, and in the end did no harm to religion. The next attempt of the theologians to thrust the Scriptures into the domain of science, was made in the case of Galileo. He was required to "abjure, curse and detest" the simple and now universally admitted doctrine that the earth revolves around the sun. Again the theologians were defeated. Astronomical science is now a fixed fact; but has it disturbed or weakened the moral truths of Revelation? Within the memory of the present generation we have another notable illustration of this dogmatism in the Church. Twenty years ago the now exploded theory was set up that God created the world in six literal days. The New York *Observer* of that period, wrote solemn and tedious editorials denouncing the wickedness of the "infidel geologists," and predicted the downfall of the Church and all true religion, from the prevalence of such doctrines. Even Chalmers and Buckland gave their assent to such a narrow interpretation of the Bible. Yet so rapid was the progress of public opinion to the truth upon this question, that the very journals that had denounced geology as an infidel science lived to praise Hugh Miller as "the Christian Geologist," though he rejected not only the "six days theory," but also the literal reading in relation to the Noachian deluge. "The conclusions to which I have been compelled to arrive," says Miller, "are, that, in exact accordance with that of the most philosophical geologists, we must accept the Mosaic days as periods—*must expect no scientific revelations in the Bible*—must receive without fear the proved facts of geology—must admit, for instance, the belief that the entire earth has not at any time, since man was made, been covered by a universal deluge."

Now we ask every candid individual whether the diversity of the origin of mankind does any more violence to the *literal* reading of the Scriptures than do the scientific deductions of astronomy or geology. The Bible is not a text book upon science, nor is it intended for any purpose where the *reason* of man can be his guide. It is a Revelation of that which was "past understanding," and which, by seeking, man could not find out! Those theologians of the present day who would strive to use the Bible to prop up their narrow and bigoted assumptions as to the proper relation of the different races of men, will be regarded in the future as belonging to the same class as those who assailed geography, astronomy and geology with their ecclesiastical anathemas. Brushing aside, therefore, the theological cobwebs with which this question is surrounded—entirely ignoring those who, as Cicero says, "*damnant quod non intelligunt*," condemn things they do not understand, the writer submits the following propositions:

First. That man-*kind*, like all other forms of creation, is composed of different species—the same as the bird-*kind*, the beast-*kind*, the fish-*kind*, &c.

Second. That there are at least six well-defined *kinds*, species, or races of men, viz: The Caucasian, or white race, the Mongolian, the Malay, the American Indian, the Esquimaux, and the Negro.

Third. That there may be slight modifications of the original types of each of these races, resulting from climates, governments, conditions of existence, temporary mongrelism or miscegenation; but as an invariable rule, each is produced after its kind as regularly as pigeons from pigeons, robins from robins, swine from swine, or dogs from dogs.

The present generation is sunk in profound ignorance, as to the proper relation of the human races. The mass of mankind is now, in reference to this question, in precisely the condition that our ancestors were, in the time of Columbus and Galileo, in regard to geography and astronomy. This ignorance is the real cause of the present horrible war, with its inevitable train of sufferings, misery, and debt. But we are learning. Out of the Red Sea of blood we shall strike solid gronnd, and though humanity will drop a tear over tho terrible cost of the education we are receiving, yet when acquired, every Miriam in the land will be justified in tuning the sweetest songs of rejoicing in honor of the grand progress we shall have made toward understanding the laws of the beneficent Creator. Doubtless this great subject could never have been understood except by the occurrence of some grand civil convulsion, which should startle the human mind from its lethargy and stolidity. The opinions of men run in grooves and channels. They are absorbed in money making, and allow a few to think for them. It requires something to throw them out of the beaten tracks. The dogma of a single human race is one of those channels—one of those beaten tracks in which the minds of men have run. As Agassiz says, "It is a theory formed in the infancy of science," yet it has been accepted as true, and from it flow all the absurd and revolting doctrines of abolitionism and miscegenation or amalgamation.

Now, upon what ground does that popular belief rest? We have shown that the Bible throws no light upon the subject, any more than it does upon geography, astronomy or geology. Historically, it deals only with the Caucasian race. It simply speaks of men and things as they existed. What do science, the laws f physiology and of anatomy say? Why, the very idea hat a negro might be the offspring of white parents is n impossible conception to the mind? The most deuded abolitionist in the land would not believe such thing possible if it were sworn to by a thousand witesses. It is now nearly three hundred and fifty years ince the negro was brought to this country, and yet o such an occurrence has ever taken place. Negroes rom negroes, and whites from whites, have been just as nvariable and as regular as dogs from dogs, or horses rom horses. Each after its kind, is as uniform a law in he human species as in those of the lower animals. But some eminent men, Dr. Prichard, for instance, who s the great luminary of the single race theory, suppose hat the differences between the races are simply the esult of climate and circumstances, and that they amount only to *varieties*, and not to specific distinctions If this be so, then we ought to find children of white parents occasionally born black, and *vice versa*, for it is well known that there is a natural tendency in all *varieties* to return to the original type. The difficulty of keeping up particular breeds of pigeons or rabbits is well known, and in all crossings of different species the tendency to return to the primitive type is manifest. Van Amringe says, "that time does not alter species is proved by the mummies of animals found in the catacombs of Egypt, and the representation of species, identical with existing ones, on the walls of the temples and the outer cases of human mummies." But if climate can change a white man into a negro, or *vice versa*, thus producing specific distinctions lasting through centuries and even ages, why adhere to the idea that man was *created* at all? Would it not be more rational to suppose that he was "developed" as held by Lamarck, or that his progenitor was a monkey, as asserted by Monboddo? But all these speculations are mere fanciful mental chimeras. It has been proved by the researches of Morton, Champollion and Rosellini that four thousand years of civilization have not changed man. Of ninety-eight Egyptian crania examined by Dr. Morton, eighty-four belonged to the unmixed Caucasian race, thirteen were mulattoes, and one a negro. And yet the author of "Miscegenation" has the hardihood to assert that "among the mummies are found all varieties except the pure white!" Can boldness and recklessness go further? As relates to animals, though they are much more susceptible of external influences than man, the same remarks will apply. In Layard's plates of Nineveh are represented the camel and dromedary just as distinct as they now are. These date as far back as 2,600 years before Christ. It is well known that the reindeer of Lapland do not change in the slightest particular even after long domestication. The peacock has not changed since Solomon went on his triennial voyages to Ophir and Tarshish. Domestication, it is true, produces great improvement in some animals, as the horse, hog, sheep, &c., but none that destroys the type of the species. If man, then, has undergone a change from the Caucasian to the African type, and degenerated to the condition of even the Bushman, why have not well-defined species of animals changed?

But there are no proofs of any changes of types, either in man or in the lower animals. Four thousand years ago the negro and the white man were physically and mentally in structure just what they now are. Seventeen hundred years ago, a colony of Jews emigrated to the coast of Malabar, and settled among the negroes. Dr. Buchanan, in his travels, says they are just as perfect

Caucasians as ever. The Moors have inhabited Northern Africa from time immemorial, and yet they have made no approach to the negro, any more than the negro has to them. The Indian of our own country, under every variety of climate and condition, preserves his own peculiar type. No fact in history is better attested than this uniformity of the different races. White men have been white men; negroes have been negroes; Mongols have been Mongols from first to last. They have resisted all the supposed causes of change, and may be considered *permanent*. The negro cannot change his skin, nor the leopard his spots.

Many people erroneously suppose that the white race were originally barbarians, and frequently compare its former condition with that of the negro, as a race, now. Nothing could be more irrational. Except that, as in all ages, some branch of the white race has been more advanced in learning or science than other branches, there has been no change. In other words, the relative differences between white men now are as great as they have ever been. The men of Abraham's time were endowed with the same faculties and the same abilities as the men of the present day. The Greeks and the Romans, in poetry and eloquence, were equal if not superior to the men of our own time, showing that the average intellect of the white race has always been the same. It was common for ancient nations to call other people barbarians. It was a kind of vanity, not yet extinct, for a people to think that they constituted "the smartest nation in all creation," and were the depositories of all the virtue, all the religion and all the knowledge that existed. The Egyptians thought so. The Greeks, and then the Romans, thought so; but there is no doubt that the Goths who swept down on Rome, were vastly the superior of her debauched and depraved population, in all the manly virtues of a true civilization. In one marked respect the Caucasian differs from all other races of men. It has the power of progression in knowledge. One generation accumulates it and transmits it to the next. It is the only race that has a progressive civilization. The Mongol stands still, after reaching a certain point. The African is invariably a barbarian unless placed in a position of subgenation and thus domesticated.

Having shown that the races were originally diverse, and that they have preserved that diversity through all vicissitudes of time or circumstance, let us examine a few of the *specific* characteristics of the negro. It is a great mistake to suppose that it is only in color that the negro differs from the white man. In figure, hair, features, language, senses, brain, mental faculties, moral powers, down even to the very elementary particles of his blood, he is as distinct from the white man as the horse from the ass, or the camel from the dromedary. In color he is black. His figure is stooping, and his gait shuffling. His hair is curly or "woolly," and eccentrically elliptical or flat; while that of the white man is straight and oval. His features are forbidding: a flat nose, enormous lips, protuberant jaws, and a face a dead blank, incapable of representing those emotions of the soul that shine through the transparent skin of the Caucasian, and which Blair calls "the chief beauty of the countenance." As to language, no negro ever did or ever can speak the language of the Caucasian until his vocal organs are re-created. It is simply a physical impossibility; as much so as it would be for the horse to change his neigh, the tiger his growl, or the dog his bark. Any one well acquainted with negroes can always detect them by their voice alone. The senses of sight and smell in the negro are stronger and much more acute than in the white man. He can detect the presence of snakes by smell alone. All nerves corresponding to animal functions, are larger than in the white race. His sight is seldom impaired. On the contrary, all his nerves of sensibility are *smaller* than those of the Caucasian. Dr. Mosely, in his "Treatise on Tropical Diseases," says: "Negroes are devoid of sensibility to a surprising degree. They are not subject to nervous diseases. They sleep sound in every disease, nor does any *mental disturbance* ever keep them awake. They bear chirurgical operations much better than white people, and what would be almost insupportable pain to a white man a negro would almost disregard." Those tender-hearted white people who judge negroes by themselves should remember what Dr. Mosely says. As to the negro brain, it is established by physiologists that it is ten or fifteen per cent. less than that of the white man, and that the posterior portion, the seat of the animal faculties, is much larger in proportion than the anterior part, the seat of intelligence. It is a general law, governing men as well as animals, that as you ascend in the scale of intelligence the posterior portion decreases, while the anterior increases. Of the truth of this law the negro is a remarkable and striking example.

As to the mental ability of the negro, it is only necessary to point to his history. With the same opportunity to advance in civilization that the white man has had, he has remained a savage. Egyptian and Carthagenian civilization flourished for hundreds of years on the continent of Africa, and yet the negro never learned the arts or sciences. It is folly to say that his condition in this country has prevented his progress; for the simple fact is undeniable that the four millions in subgenation before the war occurred were the most civilized and the best educated of any similar number of their race on the face of the earth, either now or at any former time in the world's history. The negro has invented nothing, written nothing, and, by himself, produced nothing. In morals and religion he is a savage of the first water, worships snakes or images of mud, and propitiates his gods by the brutal butchery of his own offspring! If all the distinctions we have enumerated do not show a *specific* diversity from the white race, what would Abolitionists have in order to prove it?

The author of "Miscegenation" cites Professor Draper as standard authority. The Professor's luminous work on "Human Physiology" is almost as valuable a treatise on that subject as Adam Locke's remarkable pamphlet on the geography of the moon! We give one specimen, and only one. He says: "Wherever we look upon man, he is *the same.* Stripped of exterior covering, there is in *every* climate a *common* body and a *common* mind. Are not all of us liable to the *same* diseases?" According to this abolition "philosopher," men in China are identical with those in Great Britain, or the people in Timbuctoo are precisely similar to the fashionable denizens of Fifth Avenue. "All are liable to the *same* diseases," though every expedition into the interior of Africa has been attended, if not with positive death, with frightful mortality! The malaria that kills the white man is health to the negro; and yet a man talks about the same diseases. *No negro has ever had the yellow fever* in our Southern States. So says Dr. Nott, of Mobile, who, in a practice of fifty years among them, never saw but one case where the symptoms were of the yellow fever type. As the very name implies, it is a white man's disease. A black man with a *yellow* fever; what a paradox! Professor Draper's speculations evidently belong to the domain of Cosmas' cosmogony of the earth, or Turrettine's sermon against the science of astronomy!

The facts we have cited prove beyond question the diversity of the races. Beginning with Agassiz there is probably no living naturalist who would hazard his name or fame by avowing that all men came originally from a single pair, any more than he would assert that all birds or all quadrupeds came from a single pair, or that all trees, plants or shrubs originated from a single species.

But throwing aside all speculations, pro or con, we would prefer to rest our argument for the diversity of mankind upon the simple, unperverted, common sense view of the subject. We see all about us negroes succeed negroes just as invariably as whites succeed whites; just as invariably as pigeons from pigeons, sheep from sheep, owls from owls, eagles from eagles. The idea that an owl can come from a pigeon, or an eagle from a robin is no more irrational than that a white parent can produce a negro child. We have a right to suppose that this has always been so, since creation began, unless some good reason can be shown why God has miraculously interfered to alter it. The human races were unquestionably created in their respective centres of existence, and adapted to different degrees of latitude, just as animals and plants are. This is simple common sense. It is also science. No such a silly idea as that all men descended from a single pair could have been imposed upon the human mind, had not narrow-minded ecclesiastics assumed that it was necessary to believe this in order to believe the Bible! The text, "And He hath made of one blood all nations of men," so simple, so truthful, they have twisted entirely out of its obvious meaning. Men are created of "one blood," and so are birds, that is of one type, one genus; but all birds are not owls, nor all eagles pigeons. So of man; the *genus homo*, is one type, all are human, but white men are not, therefore, negroes, nor Indians Chinese, nor ought reasonable or sensible people to expect them to perform the same duties, or exhibit the same faculties, any more than the ox is expected to possess the fleetness of the horse, the mastiff to have the exquisite sense of smell that the hound possesses, the raven to sing like a canary bird, or the owl to soar aloft with the proud and imperial eagle and gaze at the sun at noon-day! Each race is distinct—the white standing at the top, the negro at the bottom of the column. THE PROBLEM *of civilization is the harmonious adaptation of these distinct races to the purposes of human advancement.* It is expressed in one word, SUBGENATION—the normal relation of the races. It is to embody in social science the laws which the Creator has stamped on the organism of mankind.

> " Far as creation's ample range extends
> The scale of sensual, mental power ascends:
> Mark how it mounts to man's imperial race,
> From the green myriads in the peopled grass:
> What modes of sight betwixt each wide extreme,
> The mole's dim curtain, and the lynx's beam;
> Of smell, the headlong lioness between,
> And hound sagacious on the tainted green;
> Of hearing, from the life that fills the flood,
> To that which warbles through the vernal wood!
> The spider's touch, how exquisitely fine,
> Feels at each thread, and lives along the line:

In the nice bee, what sense so subtly true,
From poisonous herbs extracts the healing dew?
How instinct varies in the grovelling swine,
Compared, half-reasoning elephant, with thine?
Twixt that and reason what a nice barrier:
Forever separate, yet forever near!
Remembrance and reflection how allied;
What thin partitions sense from thought divide?
And middle natures, how they long to join,
Yet never pass the insuperable line!
Without this just gradation, could they be
Subjected, these to those, or all to thee?
The powers of all subdued by thee alone—
Is not thy reason all these powers in one?"

II.

MISCEGENATION; OR, THE MIXTURE OF THE RACES.

Owing to the limited knowledge of anthropological science, the word "race" has been used very loosely and indiscriminately. Strictly speaking, a race is a species. "A *species*," says Buffon, "is a constant succession of iudividuals similar to and capable of producing each other." "A *species*," says Cuvier, "is a succession of individuals which reproduces and perpetuates itself." Now there are just as many races as there are distinct species, and no more. The word, however, instead of being applied in this way, is often used as follows: the German race, the Anglo-Saxon race, the Spanish race, etc. This use of the word is manifestly improper; for the Germans, Anglo-Saxons, etc., are but families or varieties of the great Caucasian race, and not distinct species. How many species of men there are it is very difficult, in the present state of anthropology, to determine. The writer has taken the generally received assumption of modern naturalists, and placed the number at six, viz.: the Caucasian or white race, the Mongolian, the Malay, the American Indian, the Esquimaux, and the Negro. There are at least this number. An extended knowledge of the question of races may determine that there are more. Each of these races is subject, to a certain extent, to external influences, which produce slight modifications. The person brought up in luxury, whose hands are always covered, when he steps out, with the finest kids, and whose face is protected from the rays of the sun, presents a very different appearance from the back-woodsman, whose bronzed face and brawny hands and arms indicate constant contact with the sun, the wind, and the rain. This marked distinction occurs in the same latitude; but every person knows that it is only external and artificial. These artificial distinctions, however. become more marked as individuals of the same race are placed under different climates and different governments; but however great they may be, they can never be more than merely artificial. They are such distinctions as we see between the English, the Irish, the Germans, the French, etc., all of which disappear in this country in one or two generations. These, then, are but *varieties* of the *same* race, and not distinct species.

And the simple physiological law running through all forms of organic life is this: *The mixing of varieties of the same race improves the offspring, while the mixing of distinct species produces an inferior type, which, if not at once a hybrid, rapidly tends to extinction.* What, therefore, the author of "Miscegenation" says concerning the mixing of French, German, Danish, Saxon, and

Russian bloods is emphatically and precisely true, while everything that he asserts in relation to the mingling of *distinct* races is emphatically and precisely false. Every farmer and stock-raiser knows the importance of "crossing" varieties of the same species, and the laws of the human organism are not dissimilar in this respect from those governing the lower animals. "Crossing" improves the breeds of domestic animals, just as the intermingling in America of all varieties of the white race, makes the American white man the exponent of the vital energies of all the different varieties—thus developing an enterprise and an activity unknown in the old communities. But this is not "Miscegenation." This word the author of that work derives from *miscere*, to mix, and *genus*, a race; hence it is the mixture, not of varieties of the *same* race, but of distinct races. While, therefore, the present writer fully indorses the former, he can command no language to express his detestation of the latter.

The reader, in order to grasp fully the enormity of the latter proposition, has only to remember that the Creator "has made every living thing after its *kind*"—that is, he has stamped upon every created being a definite and distinct organism peculiar to its *kind* or species. It follows that if man could unmake or mar the works of the Great Creator, he would be as great as God himself. In the lower animals, the Creator has placed an unerring instinct which confines each to its own species, and thus preserves the integrity and organism of the race intact. To man He gave free will and reason. He can, therefore, debauch and destroy himself by violating God's laws; but he cannot alter them. If he could change, by so much as even one particle the facts fixed by the creative wisdom of the

Almighty, it would be within his power to strike worlds from their spheres, or hurl systems upon systems. That which Abolitionists call a "foolish prejudice" against negroes is a God-implanted instinct, running through all forms of creation, to preserve intact its own distinctive organism. In man, it is well known that all the natural and healthy instincts can be debauched; hence this "prejudice" can, to a certain extent, be destroyed. Let us see what Miscegenation has done in the world.

The Egyptian is believed to have been the oldest civilization. The country was undoubtedly settled, as Carthage is known to have been at a later day, by Caucasian emigrants from Asia Minor. Egypt rose to the highest pinnacle of ancient civilization. Greece and Rome borrowed their learning and many of their treasures of art from the Egyptians. But it is well known that this greatness was achieved during the austere and earlier period of their history. So far from their being "a composite people"—that is, a mongrel people —as the author of "Miscegenation" asserts, the eminent Dr. Morton, in his "*Crania Ægyptiaca,*" says "that there is abundant evidence that the complexion of the Egyptians did not differ from that of other Caucasian nations in warm latitudes. While the higher classes, protected from the sun, were comparatively fair, the lower classes were dark, and might be called black by the Greeks in comparison with their own. We find a similar variation in the modern Hindoos." During their earlier history, the Egyptians seem to have known nothing of the negro race, for it does not figure on the monuments until in connection with the military campaigns of the eighteenth dynasty.

After this the monuments give ample evidence of the

existence of subgenation, or slavery so-called, among the Egyptians. But there arose Miscegenationists in those days, and the Egyptians mingled their blood with the inferior races among them, only to fall under the withering curse of God. There is abundant evidence to show that the human mind can scarcely conceive of the bestiality in which this involved the Egyptians. Their degradation and loss of manhood made them an easy prey to the power of some pure branch of the Caucasian race. Hence Ezekiel prophecies "that Egypt shall be given to the King of Babylon," and it is still more remarkable that Ezekiel is commanded to prophesy expressly against "all the mingled people"—the miscegenationists of that day—the Beechers, the Phillipses, the Tiltons of the reign of Pharaoh-Hophra. In one place he speaks of a class of people in Egypt whose "flesh is as the flesh of asses," showing that even at that early day it was known that mongrels were hybrids, like the mule. Herodotus relates the most revolting instances of debauchery during this period of Egyptian history. Men and women lost all sense of shame; their temples even were decorated with the symbols of their debauchery, while the horrible crime of beastliness was not uncommon to this "mingled people," these "type men" who were the representatives of all that was vile, and ungodly. The Egyptians perished from miscegenation, from mongrelism, and were blotted out from the face of the earth for violating God's laws of races.

The Carthagenians are another example of the same character. They came from Tyre, and were the commercial people of those days—the Yankees of the Mediterranean. There is much in their history that resembles the rule of the Yankee dynasty in this country.

The first war they engaged in was to free themselves from the tribute which they had engaged to pay to the Aborigines or the owners of the soil, for the territory which had been ceded to them. This they succeeded in doing. In other words, they resolved that "the earth belonged to the saints, and that they were the saints." Ill success in war was a crime they never forgave. A general who lost a battle was almost sure to be killed. "Punic faith" originated with them. They belonged to the "higher law" party, broke treaties, constitutions, laws, etc., when their interests seemed to dictate it. In victory they were unrelenting and cruel, and would refuse to offer any terms of peace, or listen to any negotiation. In defeat they were crouching and servile. When Agathocles "carried the war into Africa," so sure were they of defeating him, that when they left their capital to meet him they took twenty thousand manacles for the prisoners. But they were defeated, and the manacles fell into the hands of Agathocles. This is the first Bull Run on record! But the Carthagenians, like the Egyptians, became miscegenationists. They mingled their blood with that of the negro tribes on their borders, and the result was the same decay and debauchment. They in their turn were conquered by the Romans, a pure branch of the Caucasian race, and their country laid waste. And now, of the millions upon millions of white men who have existed on the northern part of the continent of Africa, scarcely a semblance of their civilization exists. Three hundred Christian Bishops once met in convention on the site of ancient Carthage, before London was known. Now there is scarcely a remnant of Christianity or civilization left. The whole white population was first engulphed in a sea of mongrelism, and this, having a certain limited existence, perished, killing or blotting out the lesser white element, while the stronger returned to the original type. Thus are nations punished for the unnatural and beastly crime of miscegenation.

But we are not compelled to confine our proofs of this to ancient times. The Creator has spoken to this people even more distinctly than to any other. South of us "miscegenation" has been fully tried and the "sublime type of man" has not yet been produced. In Hayti, for instance, where the whites were comparatively few, the population is rapidly going back to the typical African. In the Northern States, where the negro is the feebler element, the contrary is the case. In Boston the number of births among the negro and mongrel population is not equal to the deaths. Mexico, perhaps, furnishes the most emphatic and conclusive proof on this subject. If "the type man is a miscegen," he surely ought to have been produced in Mexico. If the mixed races are superior, why is it that Mexico has been constantly declining ever since she practised miscegenation, until now a mere handful of pure Caucasians conquers her whole country. "The negro element has been grafted on the white stock" in Mexico, and "the rich treasures of blood it has vouchsafed us" are petty guerilla chiefs, and at the highest cut-throat despots, who talk of "God and Liberty" only to cover the vilest rascality. It is no wonder the country is easily overrun by a few brave Frenchmen. Like all miscegenated people from the days of the Egyptians, the Mexicans fell a prey to the arms of some pure branch of the Caucasian race. The United States committed an unpardonable sin that they did not retain possession of the country when they held it, and, restoring subgenation there, prepare it gradually for a Democracy.

It is worthy of note that the sincere Abolitionists, who have been led by the single-race theory into the errors which inevitably flow from it, are beginning to see these truths, dimly as yet perhaps, but not the less surely. The eminent Dr. Howe, of Boston, whose sincerity no one who knows him will call in question, in a report, as one of the Freedman Inquiry Commission, referring to the negro population in Canada, says: "That the negroes of Canada, being for the most part hybrids, are not of robust stock, and are unfavorably affected by the climate; that they are infertile, and that their infertility is increased by intermarriage with each other; and, therefore, unless their number is kept up by immigrants from the United States, or by some artificial encouragement, *they will decrease, and disappear in a few generations.*"

This is a distinct confession that abolitionism, and its sequence, miscegenation, simply murders the negro by a slow, but sure process of physical suffering and death. From these facts it is evident that, by practising the doctrine of miscegenation in this country, it would only be a question of time when the whites would destroy the negroes, or the negroes the whites!

To what conclusion do all these facts point? Simply this: That the crossing of distinct races produces a mongrel population, which is hybrid in its character—that is, has less powers of virility, greater tendency to disease, and hence is shorter lived, and constantly tending to the extinction of the weaker element and a return to the original type of the stronger; that the condition is an abnormalism, and one of unspeakable wrong and suffering, and ought to be prohibited so far as human laws can reach it by the most severe and exemplary punishment; that it belongs to that class of "beastly crimes" which, under the Jewish law, were punishable with death, and which, under our own, meet with great severity. In order to resist the growing progress of this delusion, we should lose no time in restoring *subgenation* all over the continent, in order to save our civilization from that overthrow which has befallen every other nation that has practised it. If we do not, the time may come when this depopulated region shall be, in the language of Paine, "as desolate as its original wilderness; the revegetating forest may cover the ruins of our cities, and the savage return from the mountains and rear his tent in the abode of our forefathers." Then will commence that political millennium in which abolitionists and wolves shall nightly chant their barbarous orgies over the downfall of American civilization!

The author of "Miscegenation" cites Tennyson as indorsing his monstrous doctrine, as follows:

"I will take some savage woman; she shall rear my dusky race;
Iron-jointed, supple-sinewed, they shall dive and they shall run,
Catch the wild goat by the hair, and hurl their lances in the sun;
Whistle back the parrot's call, and leap the rainbows of the brooks,
Not with blinded eyesight poring over miserable books."

But the unfairness of this quotation is manifest when the lines that follow the above are quoted. In a moment of despair the hero of Locksley Hall utters the above words, but at once reproaches himself, and bursts forth with the following, as grand and noble utterance as ever fell from mortal pen:

"Fool, again the dream, the fancy! but I *know* my words are wild,
But I count the gray barbarian lower than the Christian child.
I, *to herd with narrow foreheads*, vacant of our glorious gains,
Like a beast with lower pleasures, like a beast with lower pains!
Mated with a squalid savage, what to me were sun or clime?
I, the heir of all the ages, in the foremost files of time,

I, that rather held it better men should perish one by one,
Than that earth should stand at gaze like Joshua's moon in Ajalon!
Not in vain the distance beacons. Forward, forward, let us range.
Let the great world spin forever down the ringing grooves of change.
Through the shadow of the globe we sweep into the younger day;
Better fifty years of Europe than a cycle of Cathay."

III.

THE FUTURE OF THE RACES.

Having shown that there are diverse races, or species of mankind, and that the mingling of these distinct species inevitably leads to social decay and national suicide, it may not be amiss to glance at a possible, nay, a certain, future, wherein the great question, as to the proper relation of these different races to each other, shall be correctly solved. Poets have dreamed of a Utopia, in which men emancipated from their burdens were to enjoy the full fruition of their faculties. The philosopher, the political economist, and the philanthropist, have all suggested schemes intended to accomplish this long-looked-for and desired result. Fourier thought he had struck the key-note of human longings when he presented his beautiful theory of social science. Thousands of true lovers of humanity became deeply imbued with his sentiments. We have not lacked sincere and genuine philanthropists in this age of the world so much as intelligent ones, and it is no more than justice to say that the noblest and most self-sacrificing of these men are among the Abolitionists. They are straining their eyes to catch a sight of that undiscovered moral world yet to greet the vision of some future Columbus. But they are looking in the wrong direction! *Man's temporal redemption will come through a full understanding of the laws of subgenation.* The grand idea which is to be the savior of humanity in its *earthly* probation to the spiritual sphere, is summed up in one word—SUBGENATION.

Let us explain. Do you see that poor laboring white man at 6 P.M. on his way to his family. He has worked at hard physical labor since early morn for the miserable pittance of one dollar. He has a wife and five children, and is compelled to feed and clothe them upon his scanty wages. He has no relaxation from his toil. His muscles are constantly on the stretch, except when

"Balmy sleep, tired Nature's sweet restorer,"

is needed to recuperate his system for another encounter with his stern duties. The existence he spends is a merely animal one. His body lives; his mind is dead—undeveloped. Such a man performs a few animal functions, and is no more. The noble, intellectual, and moral nature which the Creator has stamped upon the Caucasian race remains as barren of culture as the Great Sahara Desert is destitute of verdure. Is it consistent with Divine wisdom to suppose that the Creator intended this white man, endowed as he is with all the capabilities of improvement that belong to any one of his race, for such a position as this? Can humanity rise no higher than a position in which nine-tenths live a life essentially and solely animal? Must the elements of poesy, art, eloquence, sculpture, and philosophy lie like the acorn in the sand, and bring forth no result? Every true heart instinctively answers, No! How, then, are we to have poets who shall rival Virgil and Homer, painters who shall excel Appeles, orators who shall shame Cicero and Demosthenes, and the Caucasian race be universally developed above the mere drudgery of an animal existence? The answer is plain and simple. By carrying out the normal order of creation—that is, embody in the civil laws of society the natural laws and ordinances of the Creator. But it may be asked, How are these to be discovered? We answer: As man has acquired all his knowledge by reason and experience. That which is found beneficial to society—to all classes—which improves and elevates, and adds to the sum of human happiness, must, in the nature of things, be *right*. The rule is one of universal application, and admits of no exception. What, then, is that normal order of creation? Why, briefly, it is to embody the natural law in the civil law—to make those who are superior by creation superior in society, and those who are inferior by creation inferior in society. The negro, as his history has abundantly demonstrated, is incapable, by himself, of civilization. In his native Africa he is a savage and a barbarian, and as useless as the horse or the ox before man caught them and domesticated them, and made them serviceable to his purposes. There is no telling the amount of labor which the horse and the ox have taken from the shoulders of mankind. In ancient times men were used for the basest drudgeries. In Layard's plates of Nineveh there are representations of hundreds of men harnessed like beasts to vast stones intended for the temples. And all the improvements of the arts have been, in modern times, tending to relieve white men from heavier and grosser labor. Could every negro now on the face of the earth be placed at useful labor, the homes of poverty would be lighted up with a smile, joy would gladden the hearthstones where sorrow, like a specter, now sits enthroned, and even the morning stars would once more sing—"joy on earth, peace and good will among men." This is no fancy dream. The elevation of humanity is to be reached by placing the races in their natural relation to each other—in a word, by subgenation.

Do not be startled, reader; but every negro in the North ought at once to be placed in a position of subgenation —that is, enslaved, as it has been called in our ignorance of the laws of races. At present, the negroes of the North are non-producers. Mr. Gerrit Smith, a few years since, tried to make farmers of them, but abandoned the experiment in despair. In a letter to Governor Hunt he said, that "the most of them preferred to *rot, both physically and morally,* in cities rather than become farmers or mechanics in the country." Even Mr. Horace Greeley confesses that, as a class, the negroes of the North "are indolent, improvident, servile, and licentious." According to the Census Reports, crimes among them are over six or eight times more frequent than among the white population. They are also rapidly perishing under the present policy, the births not being equal to the deaths. The truth is clear as noonday—God's eternal laws of subgenation are being outraged. No one has a right to try to make those equal whom God has made unequal. Never can we have a true democracy, never can humanity be elevated and ennobled, or freed from poverty and its attendant crimes, until the laws of God are respected and obeyed, and embodied in our legal and social system. *The equality of all whom God has created equal (white men), and the inequality of those He has made unequal (negroes and other inferior races), is the corner-stone of American democracy, and the vital principle of American civilization and of human progress.*

Not a moment's time ought to be lost in changing our national policy. Our armies, instead of being used as now to overthrow negro subgenation, ought to be immediately turned to fighting for it! No time should be lost in notifying foreign governments that their policy of miscegenation on this continent must come to an end at once. Then, in the face of the world, we should announce that the grand humanitarian policy of progressive and civilized America is to restore subgenation all over the American continent, from the Capes of Labrador to Terra del Fuego. We should also at once open the importation of African subgens, and defend the Christian and Democratic policy, in spite of a world of monarchists in arms. These ideas may appear startling to some people, but there are thousands of Democrats all over the North who believe in them. A distinguished shipping merchant of this city, whose name is world-wide, is a full convert to these advanced opinions, while nearly all leading Democrats, such as Charles O'Conor, C. L. Vallandigham, Fernando Wood, James Brooks, S. S. Cox and others, hold to them. Some of these gentlemen from policy may pretend otherwise, but at heart they are right. Thousands who believe them have not the courage to say so. Never was so foul a murder committed as when the true and noble young man, Gordon, was hanged in this city, in 1861, for participation in the importation of Africans. He was a martyr to ignorance and fanaticism as senseless as that which formerly hanged old women on the charge of witchcraft!

The national policy once changed, and the great laws of human progression set in motion, the entire face of society would soon be altered. This continent is the last hope of humanity. In its destiny is bound up that glorious future of which poets in all ages have dreamed, and under the operation of the race law of subgenation there is no reason why all, and even more than all, these visions might not be fully realized. And it would come in this way. The inferior races are intended by the Creator for the lower and ruder kinds of labor. It is exactly suited to their organization. The negro, for instance, has not the sense of touch so finely developed as the white race. No negress can do fine or exquisite needlework. The operation would be a physical impossibility to her fingers. The negro cannot learn the higher order of mechanic arts. No one ever heard of a negro sculptor or painter. The evident design of the Creator, therefore, is that the white race, created as it is upon a higher plane of intelligence than the negro, should be employed only in the nobler and more intellectual duties of life, while the inferior races should perform all the inferior labor, to which by their organization they are adapted. We learn the proper position of a thousand things in life from a simple understanding of the purposes they are fitted, either by nature or construction to fulfill. We have a right to apply this rule to the relation of the races. The negro rendered useful by subgenation, will make our now desert tropical region blossom like a rose. We should produce vast quantities of cotton, sugar, rice, molasses, coffee, spices, and all the articles now so exorbitantly high in price. A vast number of subgens in the tropics would form a permanent market for Northern agricultural and mechanical productions. The cost of living would soon be reduced to a merely nominal sum. Adam Smith showed, years ago, that it was not an abundance of gold and silver that men wanted, or that constituted wealth, but an abundance of the various *necessaries*, *conveniences*, and *enjoyments of life*. These we would get under this system. The advantage of being rich is that it enables men to command these enjoyments and luxuries. But we should abolish both wealth and poverty by making the enjoyments of life universal! Vain reformers! who have supposed that human progress consisted in an equal distribution of wealth! The true secret is to rob wealth of its power!

No one can estimate the amount of wealth that native Africans—now as useless as inanimate clods of clay—would produce if set to work. There is not a man so poor but could afford to own one subgen! In fact, poverty would be abolished! Almshouses would be as deserted as the Pyramids of Egypt, and prisons become as curious as the ruins of Palenque. Dr. Franklin estimated that if every white individual performed four hours' labor each day it would be sufficient for the support and maintenance of mankind. But this is altogether too high an estimate. Under the operation of subgenation, the white race would be relieved, first, of all the grosser employments, and, secondly, very much of all labor. In the far off future, it is doubtless the intention of the Creator to relieve the race created in his own image of all employment, except that which will develop the intellectual, moral, and spiritual natures. The millennium, which many people are groping in the dark to grasp, is a fact of the future; but the world is not ready for it. It was five thousand years before God revealed to Galileo the motions of the heavenly bodies. It was six thousand years before the idea of the equality of all white men was revealed to Thomas Jefferson. That idea is not yet firmly established. We, as yet, even in this country, only "see it, as through a glass, darkly," while Europe does not even acknowledge it at all. Jefferson's idea involved the proper relation of white men to white men. We have since progressed one step further, and are trying to solve the question as to the proper relation of different *races* to each other. That solved, and a new moral world, grander and more magnificent than the physical one discovered by Columbus, opens to our vision. The races placed in harmonious relations to each other, working out, each in its proper sphere, its own highest and noblest development, the real progression of society fairly commences.

IV.

THE EFFECT OF SUBGENATION UPON THE WHITE RACE.

"Falsehood," says Burke, "has a perennial spring," and never was this remark so true as in relation to subgenation. It has been attacked with a greater malevolence, and with more disregard of the virtue of truthfulness, than has fallen to the lot of any other form or order of society. Among the arguments against subgenation none has been used with more frequency than the threadbare assertion that it injures and emasculates the white race. Nothing could be more exactly the opposite of the truth. The fact is, that negro subgenation has been the means of developing the very highest type of the Caucasian man. Look at the men who inaugurated the Revolution of 1776. In what age has the world produced, taken all in all, greater or better men than Washington, Jefferson, Madison, Henry, Adams, and Hamilton? Yet all these men were the development of a society based on negro subgenation. And it is worthy of note that our greatest and most successful statesmen have been produced in that portion of the country where subgenation has been the most general, and the most firmly established. Jefferson and Jackson may be said to have been the two men whose policy has governed the country for sixty years, or down to 1861. Both were born and bred in a society founded on subgenation. The statesmen of the South have guided and controlled the government ever since its foundation, for the opposition party never held control long enough to fix their policy on the country. No one can successfully controvert this position. Indeed, the standing complaint of the Abolitionists is that the South has controlled the government ever since its formation, and that it was high time they gave it up and allowed the North an opportunity to show its statesmanship. Well, they have tried, and what statesmanship!

There is another remarkable fact. Ever since the North abolished subgenation, her statesmen have been slowly but surely degenerating. The Revolutionary era, and the era immediately succeeding it, produced Hamilton, Jay, Adams, Ellsworth, George Clinton, De Witt Clinton, Webster, and Marcy. But who have we now? Why, a Sumner, a Wilson, a Wade, a Chandler, a Seward, and Judge Busteed! Statesmen we have none; charlatans plenty. We search in vain in the ranks of all parties North for a high order of intellectual and moral dignity, or for even a breadth of view at all commensurate with the greatness and destiny of our country. Both are beyond their comprehension. We even lack simple honesty. Everywhere vice and corruption stalk abroad, like a pestilence.

Patriotism is eaten up of avarice, justice is subverted, and reason dethroned. As Pope expresses it, in his epilogue to the Satires :

> " In soldier, churchman, patriot, man in power
> 'Tis avarice all, ambition is no more ;
> See all our nobles begging to be slaves !
> See all our fools aspiring to be knaves !
> All, all look up with reverential awe
> At crimes that 'scape or triumph o'er the law,
> While truth, worth, wisdom, daily they decry,
> Nothing is sacred now but villany !"

The Peace-men and the Abolitionists are the only honest men left. Those trying to be conservatives are either false to their convictions or else only so much drift-wood, forced into the current that runs the swiftest. C. L. Vallandigham, with the blood of Virginia and Maryland running in his veins, and a strong believer in subgenation, is a bright spot on a dismal background of weakness or cowardice. The majority fiddle while a nation is dying !

There was no such universal faithlessness to principle before subgenation was overthrown. A sturdy, inflexible honor, and a genuine Roman dignity, were the characteristics of our public men down to 1820. Since then, Northern men have been degenerating. Not so, however, at the South. This war has proved how false are all the stories that negro subgenation emasculates the white race. How Virginia was sneered at for her degeneracy ; but how grandly has she rebuked her slanderers ! The mother of statesmen and Presidents ! when has she ever appeared more worthy of the mantle of Grecian or Roman bravery ? Where such unconquerable valor or such consummate statesmanship ? Even her strongest opponents concede this. The Rev. Dr. Bellows recently paid a public tribute to Virginia, more glowing than the writer might hope to equal. The Rev. Henry Ward Beecher says: " We are free to say that we cannot repress our admiration of the conduct of the Southern people in this terrible struggle. * * They have given up all for what they regard as their country. They have relinquished luxuries, submitted to hardships, suffered bereavements and losses, not only without murmuring, but eagerly; and after two years of trials that may be said almost to have revolutionized the interior of Southern society, and reduced them to the minimum of comfort, they are undiscouraged. They are even more fierce and bitter than ever."

Such unconquerable determination denotes a high order of character. But again, how vastly has the South exceeded the North in soldiership! We have produced no such men as Lee, Jackson, Beauregard, or Johnston. No such statesmen as Davis and Stephens. The logic of facts is inexorably against us, and the candid men of all parties confess it. It is also a singular fact that every new idea that this war has developed in the way of improved military strategy, or warlike invention, has come from men surrounded by subgenation. They first startled the world with iron-clad vessels, and sunk a wooden frigate as a workman would knock in pieces a glass house. They have now a sub-marine torpedo, of whose construction even, we are profoundly ignorant! Stonewall Jackson startled us by a celerity of military movement of which even Napoleon had no conception. Surely, such a people are not degenerating.

No more conclusive evidence could be given than this war has afforded, of the superiority of that form of society where subgenation exists over that where miscegenation is in tho ascendant. It develops a higher order of men, a nobler love of liberty; and from the very foundation of our country, wherever the principle of subgenation has been the most firmly fixed, there has been the sternest bravery, the highest virtue, the strictest integrity, and the most self-sacrificing devotion to liberty. In the State of South Carolina there has never occurred a divorce; nor has such a thing as bribery or corruption ever been known in her Legislature! However people may account for these *facts*, they exist and have not escaped the attention of reflecting and profound minds. Edmund Burke, with that remarkable genius which penetrated even the subtlest of human mysteries, in his speech in Parliament in opposition to the coercion of the Colonies, thus expressed himself. "There is, however," said Mr. Burke, "a circumstance attending these (the Southern) Colonies, which, in my opinion, makes the spirit of liberty still more high and haughty than in those to the northward. It is, that in Virginia and the Carolinas they have a vast multitude of slaves. Where this is the case, in any part of the world, those who are free are by far the most proud and jealous of their freedom. Freedom is to them not only an enjoyment, but a rank and a privilege. * * The *fact* is so, and those *people of the Southern Colonies are much more strongly, and with a higher and much more stubborn spirit, attached to liberty than those to the northward.*"

Subgenation, or slavery so-called, therefore, in its effects upon the white race, instead of deteriorating it, is the very means of developing all the highest attributes that can give honor or glory to mankind.

V.

SUBGENATION, THE BASIS OF DEMOCRACY.

If we look a little more closely into the philosophy of the ideas which we are considering, we shall see that the presence of diverse races in America gave birth to the very conception of democracy, and has upheld and sustained it ever since. Why is it that the States wherein the subgenation of the negro has mainly existed, have been the pioneers of democratic ideas? Mr. Jefferson, the resident of a subgen state, was the first to enunciate the great truth of white equality. Is it not self-evident that the presence of an inferior race gave him a clearer conception of the proper relations of the white race? Those whom God had created alike—that is, equal—were, of course, entitled to like or equal rights. Equal rights followed, as a logical sequence, from an equal creation. And it is somewhat remarkable that this very idea appears in the first or original draft of the Declaration of Independence. The language is as follows: "We hold these truths to be self-evident that all men are created equal, that *from that equal creation they derive*," etc. The words in italics are stricken out of the Declaration as it now stands; but it is evident that the idea floating through Jefferson's mind—not, perhaps, fully or distinctly appreciated—was that all who were *created* equal were, by virtue of that *equal* creation, entitled to equal or like rights. The silly idea, that Mr. Jefferson intended to include negroes in the phrase "all men," belongs to that class of preposterous partisan assertions which ought to cover the faces of those who indulge in them with shame and confusion forever. Aside from its inconsistency, it is evident that Mr. Jefferson never entertained any idea of the so called freedom of the negro which was not accompanied with his removal. He explains this fully in his "Notes on Virginia." Among the reasons against their remaining he gives "*the real distinctions which nature has made.*" He cites many of these, showing "a *difference* of race," and declares that "never yet could I find a black that had uttered a thought above the level of plain narration." But what is still more remarkable is the almost positive proof that this great man, with that profound sagacity for which he was distinguished, grasped the idea of subgenation, although at that time even scientific men supposed that two or three centuries could alter the original physiognomy of a race. He says: "To our reproach it must be said, that though for a century we have had under our eyes the races of black and of red men, they have never yet been viewed by us as subjects of *natural history.* I advance it, therefore, as a suspicion only, that the blacks, whether originally a distinct race, or made distinct by time and circumstances, are inferior to the whites in the endowments both of mind and *body.* It is not against experience to suppose that different species of the same genus, or varieties of the same species, may possess *different qualifications.* Will not the lover of natural history then, one who views the gradations in all races of animals with the eye of philosophy, excuse an effort to keep those in the *department of man as distinct as nature has formed them.*"

This is exactly the idea of subgenation; and it was the conception of this great and immortal truth which enabled Jefferson to enunciate, and become the great apostle of, the principles of democracy. It was the presence of the negro race, and its subgenation in accordance with nature's laws, which gave birth to this idea. The presence of the negro constantly reminded the whites how vain were all the artificial distinctions which men had engrafted upon society. It taught them the absolute natural equality of those whom God had created equal or alike—that is, of the same race, of the same species. But they saw the rules, regulations, treatment, duties, etc., in relation to the lower animals, modified, changed, and adapted to each particular species. The ox was not required to perform the duties of the horse, sheep were not expected to eat the same food as swine, the mastiff was not supposed to possess the exquisite sense of smell of the hound, nor were any one of these animals regarded as capable of exhibiting the peculiarities of the other. The rights of each were such as naturally resulted from its organization; but there *must* be absolute equality among those of the same species. To deny this would be injustice and cruelty. The men surrounded by negroes saw distinctions in men, similar to those existing in all other forms of creation. It was, therefore, self-evident that all white men having, in a generic sense, like capacities, like wants, like habits, were entitled, of course, to like rights, like laws, and were responsible for like duties. This IDEA was democracy; it was born in a society founded on subgenation, and was made the corner-stone of a new government.

Our history shows that had it not been for this conception of Jefferson's, the Revolution of 1776 would never have been more than a simple separation from the mother country. So feebly was the idea developed in the Northern States, where there were but few subgens, that they would have re-established, after the war, substantially the same government they had freed themselves from. They fought for independence. Jefferson and the Southern States fought for something more—something nobler and grander even; they fought to establish the great principle of the equality of all white men—that one man can govern himself better than another can do it for him. Subgenation taught these truths, and in this way became the basis, the very corner-stone, of DEMOCRACY. It *was* Democracy!

VI.

WOMAN AND SUBGENATION

"If I were asked," says De Tocqueville, "to what the singular prosperity and growing strength of the American people ought mainly to be attributed, I should reply to the superiority of their women." But how came the women of America to be superior to all others? Simply as follows: The conception of the proper relation of the races developed a corresponding conception of the proper relation of the sexes. The physical, mental, and moral nature of woman was different from man's, and we adapted our laws and institutions to that difference. In Europe, females of the higher classes had been treated with justice, and even with chivalry. But here we honored the *sex*, and thereby elevated it. Every ramification of society felt its revivifying influence. In all ages the respect bestowed upon woman has been a distinguishing mark of civilization, and nowhere is this respect carried to such an extent as in the States where subgenation exists. In the North we are fast adopting the corrupting civilization of Europe, which undervalues and degrades woman. With a more delicate physical structure, she is often forced to stand in our public cars, when the very instinct of "the lords of creation," with their strong sinews and Samson-like muscles, ought to prompt them to relinquish their seats to her. Such a scene as is often witnessed in New-York—of fragile women standing while lusty men are sitting—could not take place in the South. Such occurrences are the sign of decaying virtue and civilization, and evince a loss of that chivalry, and its concomitant bravery, which ought ever to distinguish the master race of mankind.

If we overthrow subgenation we shall lose, to a great extent, the conception of the proper relation of the sexes. Already that tendency is apparent in the North. All the more pronounced abolitionists are in favor of "Female Reform," as they style their efforts to destroy the proper relation of the sexes. Prostitution is also largely on the increase, and, most astounding of all, polygamy is becoming quite prevalent! The spiritualists, of whom it is said there are 5,000,000 in the Northern States, hold generally to the doctrine of a plurality of wives. There is one residing in New-York who has both a natural and a "spiritual" wife! Civilization may be refined into barbarism! As nations become effete they seem to be left to work wickedness with greediness. Rome fell a prey to her own debauchery as much as to the arms of the Goths. Indeed, contrary to generally received opinion, the latter actually carried civilization to Rome, for the first thing they did was to abolish polygamy and the gladiatorial exhibitions. True civilization resides not in learning nor the achievements of art or science, but in obedience to nature's laws. The Goths were the husbands of one wife, and entertained a high appreciation of woman. Cæsar once took the wives of the German tribes for hostages, as the most powerful pledge of their submission. Yet even so great a man as Guizot, in his "History of Civilization," has made the mistake of ascribing the elevation of women entirely to the feudal system. The fact is, it has always existed in uncorrupted white societies, and is an instinct of the race, unless debauched and destroyed by an artificial and corrupt civilization.

In the lower races, this appreciation of women is not to be found. The New Hollander, instead of courting his wife with affection, knocks her down with his club, and carries her to his cave. The Mongols treat their women as slaves; the Indian, as beasts of burden; and the Negro butchers them at his sacrifices! Is there a man so fiendish or demented as to insinuate that there can be common impulses and common affections between the sensitive and *spirituelle* white woman and such beings as these? It is an invariable law of the animal world that different species are not attracted to each other. Mungo Park relates that the African women would avoid, if possible, even the sight of a white man. In the San Domingo massacre it was not lust that drove the negroes on in their horrible butchery, but an insatiable thirst to exterminate the white *race*—the infant in its mother's arms, as well as the adult.

The very conception of love—upon which all lawful intercourse of the sexes is founded—is impossible, eternally impossible, between whites and blacks. The author of "Miscegenation," in his vile aspersions against the white women of the South, has won for his name an immortality of infamy,—should it ever come to the light,—far beyond that yet achieved by any human being. The very reason why the women of the South have been so fierce and implacable, the very reason why they have been nerved with such a lofty courage and inspired to deeds of such self-sacrificing devotion, has been because they instinctively saw that miscegenation or amalgamation *was* the object of the war, and its only logical result. While men might reach this conclusion only through the slow process of reason, the delicate susceptibility of woman grasped the idea with the speed of an electrical flash. It was the spirit born of this instinct that induced a gentle and tender Southern wife to say, "I pray that Phillip may die in the front, and that they may burn *me* on the plantation, before the Confederacy makes peace on any terms but their own." She felt that the war was for the degradation and debauchment of her sex. The destruction of subgenation would be the establishment of miscegenation, and it is this prospect which fills their souls with "a divine fury."

The author of "Miscegenation" asserts that three-fourths of the negroes of the South have white blood in their veins! A more glaring offence against truth was surely never penned. It is often asserted, and generally believed, that mulattoism is much more prevalent in the South than in the North. The fact is exactly the reverse. The Census returns show the following:

BLACK AND MULATTO POPULATION OF THE UNITED STATES.

SOUTHERN STATES.	Ratio of Mulattoes to 100 Negroes.	NORTHERN STATES.	Ratio of Mulattoes to 100 Negroes.
Alabama	7.24	California	9.94
Arkansas	16.53	Connecticut	30.51
Delaware	9.29	Illinois	85.53
Florida	10.70	Indiana	89.56
Georgia	6.21	Iowa	87.08
Kentucky	17.15	Maine	51.51
Louisiana	14.85	Massachusetts	34.80
Maryland	14.98	Michigan	76.31
Mississippi	7.01	New Hampshire	54.76
Missouri	18.67	New Jersey	18.19
North Carolina	12.06	New York	19.89
South Carolina	4.48	Ohio	129.52
Tennessee	10.88	Pennsylvania	40.07
Texas	15.73	Rhode Island	24.87
Virginia	17.84	Vermont	40.23
		Wisconsin	87.87

It is thus seen that miscegenation or amalgamation is much more prevalent in the North than in the South, and that the statements of the author of "Miscegenation" are disproved by facts and statistics. The figures show that where subgenation, as in South Carolina, is most rigidly believed in, there the races are kept the most distinct. In New England, miscegenation is undoubtedly practised more generally than anywhere else. The Western States are somewhat exceptional in this respect, and their large percentage of mulattoes is accounted for, to a great degree, by the fact that most of them have, or have had, laws excluding blacks, and the few among them are mostly of mixed blood.

It is a philosophical fact that wherever the mind of a people becomes perverted, they are liable to all sorts of excesses, and even vices. Divorce cases are more numerous in New England than in any other part of the country. The "social evil" is more widely spread there. In fact it is well known that the houses of ill-fame all over the country contain a large percentage of New England women—driven forth, as outcasts, from her factories and her schools where they became victims of her false philosophy and of her corrupting Pantheistic theology. Nowhere, indeed, is woman so degraded as where miscegenation is the most fully endorsed and practised. The recent horrible details of woman-flogging, in one of the workhouses of Massachusetts, are still fresh in public recollection. Boston, New-York, and Philadelphia swarm with the midnight reviews of their painted courtezans; and yet in New Orleans, figured in Northern imagination as a sink of sin, no such thing was known as a "street walker," before the advent of the "civilizers" and "humanitarians" from Massachusetts!

The revival of woman-whipping in New England, in the year of our Lord 1863, is an omen of startling significance, and the facts of the case are worthy of a passing notice. It appears from the Report of the House of Reformation for Juvenile Delinquents in Boston, for 1863, that a young lady, a victim of poverty, aged seventeen years, was cruelly and brutally *whipped with a rattan*, half an inch in diameter and twenty inches long, over the shoulders and back of her neck, until *her flesh was black and blue!* Here is a white girl, with all the delicate and sensitive peculiarities of her race and sex, outraged by an inhuman beating from some monster in the form of man. Such an occurrence is a proof that Nature's laws have been subverted, and that a society where such acts are allowed must be rapidly nearing that abyss of abnormalism, wherein utter ruin awaits it. But another revolting feature of this disgraceful affair is to be found in the fact that all the ordinary proprieties of life are systematically set aside in the institution referred to. The Report already alluded to, says:

"All the prisons are provided with the ordinary bath-tub, from three to seven in number, and placed side by side at a distance of from twelve to twenty-four inches apart; these are all in open rooms, *without any screen or protection whatever;* and in these publicly exposed tubs, the prisoners—*men, women, and girls*—in their respective departments, in groups of from three to seven, are required to perform their ablutions! Old offenders, young offenders, girls of nine or ten years of age, alike *must disrobe themselves in full observation of their fellows and officers, and, in a state of utter nudity, enter the bath, perform its duty,* and partake its refreshment!"

It should be remembered that the above takes place at the "hub of the universe"—in a city wherein civilization is supposed, by its amiable philosophers, to have reached its climax. This is the society, too, which Mr. Charles Sumner, in one of his magnificent flights of eloquence in the Senate, describes as "a cosmos of perpetual beauty and power!" The writer cites these facts simply to show that a departure from Nature's laws does such violence to social order that it works out a punishment in every ramification of life. When a pestilence prevails, it spares neither rich nor poor; so, when society has a gangrene at its vitals, it pervades the entire body politic.

In Fifth Avenue the number of violations of the seventh commandment is fearful. Reliable information, derived from persons who have been behind the scenes, renders it certain that there are in Fifth Avenue more husbands untrue to their wives, and more wives faithless to their husbands, than there are among a population of equal numbers anywhere in this country. The amount of infanticide is fearful. Pills to prevent maternity are in almost universal use—even in the families of clergymen. These things are unknown in the South, where subgenation has developed a higher order of womanhood. The care and comfort of her subgens give the Southern matron employment, devolve upon her responsibilities and duties, develop her character, and impart to her an ease, grace, and womanly dignity, which is, of itself, a citadel of virtue.

How base, how wicked, then, in view of all these facts, are the insinuations and statements that the South is a vast harem. No people on the face of the earth are so virtuous, taken as a whole. No where is woman more fully appreciated or more tenderly cared for. The chivalric deference paid to the sex is something unknown at the North; and if there be anything that can fill Southern man or matron with irrepressible rage, and lead at once to a bloody chastisement, it is to insinuate aught against the virtue of mother, wife, or daughter. And it is Subgenation which keeps alive, gives force and prominence, to this sentiment, develops a higher virtue, inspires a loftier courage, and makes braver men and purer women! We must readopt it in the Northern States, or we shall inevitably decline, until, given over to the monstrous debaucheries of miscegenation, we shall be eaten up of corruption!

Gibbon declares that Rome "attracted the vices of the universe," and New-York can most assuredly lay claim to an equal distinction in infamy. If the vail which conceals her depravity were drawn aside, the mind of the virtuous would start back with horror from the sight. Twenty thousand courtezans, our own sisters, are the monumental shame of this metropolis! The gorgeous temples of their sin are furnished with every embellishment which art or genius can suggest to pander to lasciviousness or excite lust. This degradation of womanhood is the most appalling fact of the nineteenth century. Where Subgenation exists there is scarcely such an instance as a white woman becoming a prostitute; and, as we have shown that Miscegenation is much less practised there, than where it does not exist, it follows that society must be infinitely more pure and virtuous in the Southern than in the Northern States. Not long since the writer received, from a medical friend, some statements in regard to vice in New York, which had come to his knowledge in a professional way. They staggered belief, and would have been rejected by him entirely had they not been so well authenticated as to admit of no doubt. The debaucheries of Sodom and Gomorrah, as related by Ezekiel, were familiar to him; he had read the accounts which Herodotus gives of the horrible beastliness of the miscegenated Egyptians; Livy's statements in relation to Carthagenian depravity was also vividly fixed in his mind, to say nothing of the Roman orgies and bachanals, which are still more familiar; and yet *all these have not surpassed, if equalled, what is constantly occurring in New York!* These words are written with a full understanding of their signification and import; the writer asserts them with the utmost confidence in their truth. These pages would not be fit for public perusal were the whole truth stated. Not long since a ball, in which the sexes were to appear *in puris naturalibus*, was broken up by the police. They are of frequent occurrence, however, and end in debaucheries too shocking to relate. Jezebel is supposed to have degraded herself to the condition of a beast, and was so inexpressibly vile that even the dogs refused to eat portions of her body. She has counterparts, however, in these days, and they are to be found precisely where people arrogate to themselves a superior virtue and morality. When ladies (!) of fashion and fortune pledge their "love and honor" to burly negroes, the taint of infection must have permeated every strata of society. We need an antidote to restore it to a healthful condition. That antidote is Subgenation, which lifts up woman, as well as the entire white race, to a higher plane of virtue and purity!

VII.

SUBGENATION AND THE PRESIDENTIAL ELECTION.

The author of "Miscegenation" says, "that when the President proclaimed emancipation, he proclaimed the mingling of the races." This is emphatically true. The real question before the country is Subgenation *vs.* Miscegenation. The great mass of Democratic politicians strive to avoid this inevitable issue; they think the people are not prepared for it; that they have been educated in the theory of a single race, and from such a premise Subgenation is wrong. But Abolitionism they admit is also wrong, while Miscegenation—though really its necessary result—they regard as monstrous. It is Scylla and Charybdis to them; hence they are in search of a political "northwest passage"—any way that shall avoid the issue the Abolitionists offer. They grow eloquent over free speech, free press, *habeas corpus*, and other side questions, until King John, his refractory barons and Runnymede, have become as familiar to us as nursery rhymes. It is apparent, therefore, that the Democratic leaders are not the antagonists of the giant of Abolitionism; they are only flies that annoy him a little as he strides on in his gigantic career of carnage. Look at Horatio Seymour—a great man, intellectually; and yet his talents are frittered away, because he does not know whether he stands on solid ground or a trembling bog. He seems to have no conscientious faith in anything; hence he drifts, drifts, drifts, until he has just about reached the camp of his opponents. What Pliny told Trajan—that "all our actions upbraid us of folly"—ought to be the epitaph on his tombstone. Edward Everett is another lamentable example of a great mind utterly undone for want of a philosophical theory of our politics. Wendell Phillips, on the contrary, adopts a theory on the question of races which he accepts as truth; he is, therefore, a positive power—is bold, aggressive, and combative. His opponents are timid, defensive, and irresolute. If men like Horatio Seymour, S. S. Cox, and James Brooks will not meet this question on its merits, if they have nothing to offer the people but the dry husks of expediency, they must be swept aside. We must get down to the hard pan of principle, or we are lost. Democracy must have no halting teachers, who "palter to the people in a double sense." A Democratic party that will not try, at least, to save Democracy, is the play of "Hamlet" with Hamlet left out. Subgenation, as we have shown, is the basis of Democracy—its very corner-stone. We must lose no time in inscribing it upon our banners for the Presidential election. The most intellectual and advanced minds in the Democratic party, like Taney, O'Conor, Vallandigham, Voorhees, and Seymour, of Connecticut, have given in their adhesion to it; nineteen twentieths of the rank and file instinctively accept it, and will joyously vote for it. But what is remarkable, the politicians do not believe this; they think everybody is deceived and deluded on the subject, except themselves! *They* are profoundly wise and sagacious. The writer, who has had an opportunity during the past winter to become acquainted with the opinions of most of the Democratic members of Congress on this question, was struck with this remarkable fact. Almost to a man they are, at heart, in favor of Subgenation (slavery). Even Messrs. Brooks and Cox do not differ, in this respect, materially, from Jefferson Davis or Alexander H. Stephens. The country, therefore, is perishing not so much for a lack of knowledge as from a want of moral courage; it is dying from sheer cowardice. At the time of the witchcraft delusions, it is now known that only about one-third of the people believed in them; but as this one-third comprised the governor of the Colony and all the divines of the day, it terrorized over the other two-thirds. A few brave men could have stayed the fury of those murderous zealots then, just as a few brave men can crush Abolitionism now; but they must hit it squarely on the head; pulling at its tail feathers will not answer.

A very plausible mode of avoiding the real issue is States Rights. "The *status* of the negro is left to each state," says the objector. True; but we are a *family* of nations, and no one member has a moral right to do that which injures, or even disgraces, a neighbor. A person cannot expect to retain his standing in society who turns liar and thief. But Subgenation is said to be the "sum of all crimes," and, if it be, how can States practising it expect to remain unmolested, any more than individuals who do wrong? An act of Congress to suspend the law of gravitation would be just as effectual as States Rights to stop the operation of the moral laws of the universe. God is not to be deceived. That which is Right will in the end succeed; that which is Wrong will go down. Even "the right of secession" does not get us out of the difficulty. Granted, to the last extreme, the right of a State to secede; and yet, owing to the fact of our Federal government being a compact, it is one of those rights which depend upon the *moral* right to exercise it. The simple truth is: A party was coming into power, pledged against Subgenation—the very basis of Southern civilization; pledged to use the government of all the States, to quote the language of one of its leaders, "to build a wall about slavery, so that it would be forced to sting itself to death." Such a party was, in every sense, the enemy of the people of the South; they so regarded it; they had the moral right to do so, and that comprehends all other rights. They simply defended themselves from the attempt to inflict upon them the vilest wrong ever conceived of since the world began—Miscegenation. God grant that they may be successful in this pious work!

But so long as the people of the North, or a considerable portion of them, believe Subgenation a sin, they will continue to make war upon it in some form; not that they desire deliberately and willfully to inflict an injury upon the South. *The danger lies in the fact that they do not know what is or is not an injury.* Ignorance of the laws of races is the great stumbling block.

"One reels to this, another to that wall;
'Tis the same error that deludes them all."

And politicians, with their nostrums, confuse and blind the people, instead of enlightening them. "Stand by the Constitution," they say, just as if Mr. Lincoln had not doubled it up and tucked it away in a pigeon hole more than three years ago. Besides, what is a constitution to masses of men inflamed by the passion that the great and glorious ends of humanity are to be subserved by the line of policy they are pursuing? The irrevocable theory of constitutions is exploded, Mr. Noodle's oration to the contrary notwithstanding. The Southern Democrats were far in advance of Northern Democrats in this respect. When they saw that an Abolitionist had been elected President, they knew that the spirit of the government was gone; the form only remained, and they cast it aside as a person would put off a dirty garment. The North,

"Pleased with a rattle, tickled wit[illegible]traw,"

has been fighting for this dead form, and for a flag—a symbol whose substance has vanished. Of the old government there is now nothing left, except its forms —the buildings at Washington, a huge pile of cannon, a few old ships, a monstrous debt, and a monument of dead men's bones! That which gave it its life has been exorcised by the evil spirits who now surround its prostrate form. Subgenation, though not expressed in distinct terms, was the life of the old government. The Supreme Court has so decided. Every President down to Abraham Lincoln has so administered it. Vice-President Stephens, of the Confederate States, therefore showed himself the wisest statesman of modern time when he declared that their new government made Subgenation, "the normal relation of the races, its corner-stone." In a word, it was explanatory of the old government—nothing more. The South is trying to perpetuate the old government as founded on Subgenation; Mr. Lincoln is trying to erect a new one founded on Miscegenation. Shall we allow him to do so? It is not a war of sections, but of ideas; it is not a question of disunion, but of principle. To meet the real issue, therefore, the Democracy must inscribe Subgenation upon its banners in the next Presidential contest. But will it be done?

Burke, in concluding his grand oration in opposition to the coercion of the American Colonies, says: "All this I know will sound wild and chimerical to the profane herd of vulgar and mechanical politicians—a sort of people who think that nothing exists except that which is gross and material, and who, therefore, far from being qualified to be directors of the great movement of empire, are not fit to turn a wheel in the machine." Unfortunately, it is "the mechanical politicians" who are now at the head of the Democratic party. They have no earnest or conscientious convictions. They see the country desolated and ruined, wealth squandered, lives sacrificed, and wrongs unnumbered daily committed, which cry aloud to Heaven for vengeance, and yet they aid the wrong-doers. Hyder Ali's desolation of the Carnatic was not more terrible than Mr. Lincoln's devastation of the South. Yet who protests? The Peace men must rouse themselves, sweep away the War leaders of the Democracy, and nominate a candidate for President who shall bear upon his banner Peace and Subgenation. This will herald not only a party victory, but vastly more—the triumph of Virtue, Civilization, and Democracy.

But suppose neither true principles nor proper candidates are nominated at Chicago, what then? Why, there is one more chance left the Radical Democracy of the North. If they are denied the privilege of seeing their own principles triumphant, they can, at least, contribute to crush the breath out of all the shilly-shally politicians, whether of the double-dealing Lincoln-Seward school, or of the inconsistent shoddy War-Democracy. General John C. Fremont is now the candidate of the logical Abolitionists, pledged to free discussion and individual rights. His Abolition principles the Radical Democracy deem abhorrent; but they prefer, next to their own success, the success of the exactly opposite. Let the real thing be revealed to the people; let principles be applied or abandoned. Do not keep the country dying by inches, bleeding at every pore, but still lingering. If perfect equality of all races and colors be life, happiness, and prosperity, let us have it; let us perish by utter ruin rather than count the tardy minutes of a sickening exhaustion. Such is the heart-impulse of the people to-day.

There is one fact not generally known, and never before published. Last fall, when the Hon. C. L. Vallandigham was running for Governor of Ohio, General John C. Fremont applied to the Democratic Committee of that State to stump the State in favor of Mr. Vallandigham's election! Shame be upon them, he was refused! General Fremont would have defended Mr. Vallandigham's right to express his opinions, and rebuked the despotic insolence of the Administration. This fact is pretty generally rumored among Peace-men, and, in case the Chicago Convention puts up men who arrest Legislatures, it will be remembered at the polls.

Hon. M. F. Conway, of Kansas, may be regarded as the exponent of Fremontism, when, in the House of

Representatives, he announced that he was willing to see "the two civilizations"—as he called Northern and Southern society—enter into a friendly competition for the march of empire Gladly would the friends of Subgenation accept this solution of our difficulties ; for, with public opinion relieved from the terrors of dungeons, and the press free from the control of bayonets, they would have all the elements of success to which they are entitled. If Subgenation cannot stand the scrutiny of discussion, it must and ought to fall. If Abolitionism cannot undergo the like ordeal, then let it be consigned to the tomb of the Capulets. The man, therefore, who stands honestly and determinedly by the sacred right of free discussion, who will demand the same privileges for others in this respect which he claims for himself, upholds the cause of Progress and Civilization. If in the throes of civil war, we can snatch only this precious right from the wreck of our system, the Future will be safe. In the final result, therefore, if the Democratic Convention proves faithless, and, as General Fremont is irrevocably pledged to the position we have indicated, it is certain that he will get the votes of the Peace men in preference to any doubtful candidate, who, having no conscientious convictions in principles of any kind, would be likely to give us a prolongation of the present dynasty of force and fraud.

VIII.

THE RECOGNITION OF THE CONFEDERATE STATES.

While the Hon. Mr. Long, of Ohio, would recognize the Confederate government in *form*, the writer would do something better ; he would recognize and accept its *principles*. This immediately fixes a basis for reunion. At the risk of even an American Bastile, the writer will not hesitate to express his deep and earnest conviction upon this important point. He who shuns to declare the whole truth in these days, is false to the instincts of manhood; while he who would strive to crush the free expression of thought belongs to the age of a Nero or a Torquemada.

> " Tyrants, in vain ye trace the wizard ring,
> In vain ye limit; minds unwearied spring;
> What? can ye lull the wingéd winds asleep?
> Arrest the rolling waves or chain the deep?
> No! the wild wave contemns your sceptred hand;
> It rolled not back when Canute gave command."

Thought, like "the wild wave," contemns the power of force, while *degeneres animos timor arguit.* In a word, therefore, the solution of our difficulties is *the adoption by the North of the Confederate Constitution!* There has not been a time since this war began when peace would not have brought about substantially this result within a period of six or twelve months. As has been shown, the Confederate Constitution is simply ours, *explained* on the question of the relation of the races. It sets at rest forever the distracting negro question in the only way that it ever can be permanently settled. Unfortunately, it retains the old and vicious nomenclature, calling subgens, slaves, and subgenation, slavery; but this can easily be remedied, and arose, not from any mistake as to the relation itself, but solely from the want of a proper word to express that relation—a want which the writer trusts he has supplied.

The intelligent leaders of the Miscegenation party see very distinctly that this is the only way by which the old Union can ever be restored, and they are prosecuting the war expressly to prevent it. Fortunately, we have distinct proof on this point. Mr. Horace Greeley, in the *Independent*, in October, 1861, held the following language: "The reconstruction of the Union on the basis of the Confederate Constitution, making slavery in substance omnipotent and universal, is the end distinctly contemplated to-day by thousands of nominal loyalists, as well as by open traitors; *such is the consummation which is prevented by a vigorous prosecution of the war for the Union.*"

Mr. Greeley is perfectly right. The war is prosecuted to prevent a restoration of the old Union. As for Subgenation becoming "omnipotent and universal," that is just what every Democrat and friend of humanity desires. The Miscegenationists have undertaken not only to revolutionize our system, but to undo nature's laws of races, *magni laboris opus*; but, like Satan, they have rebelled against God, and, like him, they will ingloriously fail.

That the people of the North would gladly accept the Confederate Constitution, as a basis of Union, there can be no doubt. Is there not an overwhelming majority in the North in favor of a government wherein white men only are sovereigns, as against one wherein negroes are participants in that sovereignty? No one will for a moment doubt it. Immediate peace and the adoption of the Confederate Constitution is the shortest and best road to reconstruction. We might drop a tear, for memory's sake, over the old government, which the Miscegenationists have polluted—nothing more; but the people would joyfully array themselves in the *pure white* Confederate Constitution, and, having sloughed off all the impurities of the present, march on to a realization of the destiny of the ages!

Doubtless the readiest *mode* of accomplishing this righteous triumph would be to nominate Mr. Jefferson Davis at Chicago, for he is the truest representative of these principles. No man is more strongly in favor of peace than he—none so fully convinced of the righteousness of Subgenation. It would also simplify the canvass. The Democracy would commence the campaign with the electoral votes of eleven States, and would only have to get the balance to elect Mr. Davis the legal President of all the States. In view of the great importance of restoring the Union, and with the sure prospect of its accomplishment in case of success, victory would be certain; provided, indeed, the people were not driven from voting freely for their choice. Some thoughtless people may think ours an extreme proposition; but, pray, what right has Mr. Abraham Lincoln to dictate to the people of this country as to who they shall vote for? If they prefer Mr. Jefferson Davis to himself, will any one versed in the mysteries of republican institutions tell us by what right they are deprived of that preference?

The South are also entitled to the President at this election. The North has had the candidate for four terms. In no other way can a Democratic candidate be elected. There never was one elected without the aid of the Southern States. There cannot be now.

But it may be said, the Convention will not *dare* to do this. Liberty, then, is surrendered at the point where fear controls action. It is no longer a Democratic party, but a sham, a deception, a set of cowards trying to sneak into office through some back-door which the party in power may have left unguarded. Away with such pigmy descendants of honorable sires. But "Mr. Lincoln will fight us if we attempt it." Will he? But have we not declared that the freedom of the ballot-box shall be preserved, though the country be deluged in blood? Let us stand up, then, to our professions and our principles, or ignominiously announce ourselves dastards and poltroons.

IX.

THE MILLENNIUM SOLVED.

Goldsmith, in his "Citizen of the World," in contemplating the sorrows and wrongs of humanity, exclaims: "Why, why was I born a man, and yet see the sufferings of wretches I cannot relieve!" It is this unsatisfied feeling which, in all ages, has given rise to that universal longing for a better time—for a realization of the ideal in the practical. But there is a philosophical reason at the bottom of this sentiment. Mankind, despite every obstacle, instinctively surges onward, toward the realization of the complete development of its physical, mental, and moral powers. The man is a representative of the race. Individuals perish; but the race lives on, and constantly progresses toward that perfection which will usher in the new era, when one can exclaim, with Pope:

"Rise, crowned with light, imperial Salem, rise!
Exalt thy towery head, and lift thy eyes!
See a long race thy spacious courts adorn;
See future sons and daughters yet unborn,
In crowding ranks on every side arise,
Demanding life, impatient for the skies!
See barbarous nations at they gate attend,
Walk in thy light, and in thy temple bend."

The idea of Subgenation is expressed in the last two lines, and is borrowed from the prophet Isaiah. It is evident that Subgenation is an indispensable prerequisite to the ushering in of the millennium, which many people erroneously suppose is the literal second-coming of Christ. Not at all; it is simply the practical application of the great principles of Democracy which he taught. The equality of all white men has been conceded; but the mistake of the age has been in supposing that that equality also applied to all other races. When this error is dissipated, and Subgenation is tho acknowledged basis of society and government, a new moral world is at once opened to view—a new era is ushered in which will produce greater changes in ethics and religion than any that has ever preceded it. Then, indeed, we shall step upon the threshold of that glorious cycle known as the Millennium, in which the grand and benign teachings of Christ—not yet even understood, much less applied—will be practicalized. This will, in effect be the second coming of Christ, when

> "He from thick films shall forge the visual ray,
> And on the sightless eye-ball pour the day."

But what is the simple philosophy of all this? The answer is obvious. Beings of the same race are created generically alike; and hence the requirement of nature is that all of the same race should approximate to an *equality of condition*. This has ever been the tendency. De Tocqueville says: "In running over the pages of history for seven hundred years, we shall scarcely find a single great event which has not promoted equality of condition. The Crusades and the English wars decimated the nobles and divided their possessions; the municipal corporations introduced democratic liberty into the bosom of feudal monarchy; the invention of fire-arms equalized the vassal and the noble on the field of battle; the art of printing opened the same resources to the minds of all classes; the post-office brought knowledge alike to the door of the cottage and to the gate of the palace. The discovery of America opened a thousand new paths to fortune, and led obscure adventurers to wealth and power. Whithersoever we turn our eyes, we perceive the same revolution going on in the Christian world. The various occurrences of national existence have everywhere turned to the advantage of Democracy; all men have aided it by their exertions, both those who have intentionally labored in its cause, and those who have served it unwittingly; those who have fought for it, and those who have declared themselves its opponents, have all been driven along in the same track, have all labored to one end—some ignorantly and some unwillingly—all have been blind instruments in the hands of God. The gradual development of the principle of equality is, therefore, a Providential fact. It has all the chief characteristics of such a fact. It is universal, it is durable; it constantly eludes all human interferences; and all events, as well as all men, contribute to its progress."

These are wise and philosophical remarks, drawn from the teachings of history, and, with an understanding of the philosophy upon which they rest, the reader will see that they are not only true, but necessarily true. The germ implanted in man must grow and expand; it must yearn after that condition of existence which shall enable it to exactly live out the life which the Creator has stamped upon its organism. This can never be done until every other being is also fitted in the place nature intended for him. Every wheel, every cog, every bolt and bar of the social machinery must be harmoniously adjusted, before mankind can realize its highest destiny, or social order be fully evolved.

> " Order, thou eye of action! wanting thee
> Wisdom works hoodwinked in perplexity;
> Entangled reason trips at every pace,
> And truth, bespotted, puts on error's face."

We are now rapidly nearing that period. The present war against Subgenation will end, one way or another, in a stupendous and deserved failure. When it ends, the glorious manhood of the South, which has bared its breast to the assaults of insensate bigotry, superstition, and ignorance, will be hailed as the typemen of the Millennium—as the glorious defenders of all that was sacred or valuable in human society. Their strong arms and brave hearts alone uphold the cause of freedom and civilization. Miscegenation is Monarchy; Subgenation is Democracy. Lincoln and his cabinet are the tools of the cunning monarchists of the Old World, who have hoped to perpetuate the reign of Antichrist by hurling Northern upon Southern Democrats. The Tories of England have always believed that the Tory element in this country would yet get hold of the government, and transform it into a monarchy. When Lincoln issued his Miscegenation Proclamation, he proclaimed a monarchy. England forced him to do it under the threat to recognize the Confederate States. France has bullied him into abandoning the "Monroe Doctrine" in the same way. In fact, however, there is no propriety in the Monroe Doctrine in the hands of the party in power; it was intended to preserve Democracy, which they would destroy. Democrats will never fight for a Monroe Doctrine which, under Abolition construction, means a burlesque republic of miscegens. Monarchy naturally follows miscegenation, and is the only power capable of evolving order out of such a social chaos.

Louis Napoleon, therefore, has a mission in Mexico. Let him work it out. Under the circumstances he will be one of those whom De Tocqueville describes as having "unwittingly aided Democracy." In due time his rule will be overthrown, and Subgenation and Democracy become the normal order of society all over the New World. The down-trodden and oppressed of every land will find here a refuge and a home. The people of Africa will be rapidly transferred from their native barbarism to civilization, and, while securing an equality of condition to their own race, will contribute to bestow the same boon on the superior race. Divines will vie with each other in preaching up this Christianizing work. All the money now expended for missionary societies will be devoted to the great and beneficent work of establishing Subgenation everywhere. In 1751 that eminently pious man, the Rev. George Whitfield, wrote in relation to bringing subgens from Africa: "I should feel myself highly favored if I could purchase a good number of them, in order to make their lives comfortable, and lay the foundation of bringing them up in the nurture and admonition of the Lord." It will not be many years before Christian ministers will repeat Whitfield's wish. If the benevolence and philanthropy of this age, now so lamentably perverted, could be enlightened and directed, the grandest and most glorious results for suffering humanity would be achieved. But, in any event, the result will be worked out; for human development admits of no defeat. The writer has already shown how the labor of millions of industrious subgens will so add to the necessaries and luxuries of life as to rob wealth of its power and influence, and realize the idea of Lycurgus—a society in which there shall be neither rich nor poor. *This equality of condition —an inevitable result from an equality of creation—is the* MILLENNIUM—that profound mystery which has puzzled prophets and mountebanks from Tertullian to Joe Smith.

X.

AN OMEN.

The writer of "Miscegenation" considers it a most providential event, and as one significant of the type-man or miscegens of the future, that the statue on the dome of the Capitol at Washington is of a "bronze tint." But it is possible that he mistakes its significance. As has been shown in these pages, the mixed or mongrel people perish, and are blotted from the face of the earth. The Egyptians, the Carthagenians, and now the Mexicans, are historical examples of God's punishment upon those who dare to mar the works of His creation. The dome of the Capitol, therefore, with its mulatto statue, has the symbol of decay upon it, and it would seem to constantly point to the triumph of the Confederate or *White* Constitution in the place of the mongrelized one which the folly of the hour has deified.

CONCLUSIONS.

In the preceding pages, the author has endeavored to make plain the following propositions, and, as they are the very reverse of those laid down by the author of "Miscegenation," he adopts the mode of that writer in summing up, in order the more successfully to present the contrast:

1. That as by the teachings of science, religion, and democracy, the human family is composed of different races or species, distinct in color and other physical as well as mental peculiarities, it follows that there should be distinctions in political and social rights, corresponding with such physical and mental differences.
2. That the doctrine of human brotherhood should be accepted in its entirety in the United States, and that it implies the equality of all whom God has created equal, and the inequality of all whom He has made unequal.
3. That a solution of the negro problem will not have been reached in this country until public opinion universally sanctions negro Subgenation.
4. That, as the negro ought not to be driven out of the country or exterminated, and as for wise purposes he has been placed side by side with the white race, there should be severe laws passed punishing any sexual intercourse between the races.
5. That the mingling of diverse races, or Miscegenation, is a positive injury to the progeny, producing a weaker and a hybrid race, which rapidly perishes, as proved by the history of all nations, from that of Egypt to this day.
6. That, as the war has been caused by the Miscegenationists striving to force their revolting and disgusting doctrines on the people of the South, it follows that perfect peace and Union can soonest be restored to our country by the North adopting

negro Subgenation at once, by each State amending its Constitution to that effect, and then accepting the Confederate Constitution as the basis of a Federal Government.

7. That it is the duty of Democrats everywhere to advocate Subgenation, or the normal relation of the races on this continent, as a great humanitarian reform.

8. That as the last Presidential election was carried by the Miscegenationists, and has brought four years of blood, suffering, and untold taxation upon the country, the next Presidential election should be carried by the Subgenationists, who will thus restore order, peace, and commercial prosperity.

9. That a society founded on Subgenation produces the highest type of mankind—the most consummate statesmen and generals, the highest type of womanhood, and the most exalted morality and virtue.

10. That the Millennial future is to be ushered in through a complete understanding of the laws of Subgenation, by which an equality of condition is to become universal—thus realizing the instinct of an equality of creation; and that whoever helps to achieve this result, helps to make the human family the sooner realize its great destiny.

APPENDIX.

From the "Testimony of the Rocks," by Hugh Miller.

Turrettine's Sermon Against the Science of Astronomy.

he second great error to which the theologians would fain have lged the truth of Scriptures was an error in the astronomical vince. I need scarce refer to the often adduced case of Galileo. doctrine which the philosopher had to "abjure, curse, and de-," and which he was never again to teach, "because erroneous, etical, and contrary to Scripture," was the doctrine of the earth's ion and the sun's stability. But to the part taken by our Pro-ant divines in the same controversy,—men still regarded as au-rities in their proper walk,—I must be allowed to refer, as less wn, though not less instructive, than that enacted by the Romish irch in the case of Galileo. "This we affirm, that is, that the h rests, and the sun moves daily around it," said Voetius, a at Dutch divine of the middle of the seventeenth century, "with divines, natural philosophers, Jews and Mohammedans, Greeks Latins, excepting one or two of the ancients, and the modern owers of Copernicus." And we detect Heideggeri, a Swiss theo-ian, who flourished half an age later, giving expressions, a few rs ere the commencement of the last century, to a similar view, om which," he states, "our pious reverence for the Scriptures, word of truth, will not allow us to depart." A still more remark-e instance occurs in Turrettine, whom we find in one of his writ-s arguing in the strictly logical form, "in opposition to certain losophers," and in behalf of the old Ptolemaic doctrine that the mosphere." The theologian, after thus laying down the law, set himself to meet the objections. If it be argued that the Scriptures in natural things speak according to the common opinion, Turrettine answers, "*First*, the Spirit of God best understands natural things. *Secondly*, That in giving instruction in religion, he meant these things should be used, not abused. *Thirdly*, That he is not the author of any error. *Fourthly*, Neither is he to be corrected on the pretence of our blind reason." If it be further argued, that birds, the air, and all things are moved with the earth, he answers, "*First*, That this a mere fiction, since air is a fluid body; and, *Secondly*, if so, by what force would birds be able to go from east to west?"

Now this I must regard as a passage as instructive as it is extraordinary. Turrettine was one of the most accomplished theologians of his age; nor is that age by any means a remote one.

Physical Differences Between the Negro and Caucasian Races.

By S. A. Cartwright, M.D., of New Orleans.

The nerves of organic life are larger in the prognathous (negro) species of mankind than in the Caucasian species, but not so well developed as in the simiadiæ. The brain is about a tenth smaller in the prognathous man than in the Frenchman, as proved by actual measurement of skulls by the French savans, Palisot and Virey. Hence, from the small brain and the larger nerves, the digestion of the prognathous species is better than that of the Caucasian and its animal appetites stronger, approaching the simiadæ, but stopping short of their beastiality. The nostrils of the prognathous species of mankind open higher up than they do in the white or olive species, but not so high up as in the monkey tribes. In the gibbon, for instance, they open between the orbits. Although the typical negro's open high up, yet owing to the nasal bone being short and flat, there is no projection or prominence formed between his orbits by the bones of the nose, as in the Caucasian species. The nostrils, however, are much wider, about as wide, from wing to wing, as the white man's mouth from corner to corner, and the internal bones, called the turbinated, on which the olfactory nerves are spread, are larger and projects nearer to the opening of the nostrils than in the white man. Hence the negro approximates the lower animals in his sense of smell, and can detect snakes by that sense alone. All the senses are more acute, but less delicate and discriminating than the white man's. He has a good ear for melody, but not for harmony; a keen taste and relish for food, but less discriminating between the different kinds of esculent substances than the Caucasian. His lips are immensely thicker than any of the white race, his nose broader and flatter, his chin smaller and more retreating, his foot flatter, broader, larger, and the heel longer, while he has scarcely any calves at all on his legs when compared to an equally healthy and muscular white man. He does not walk flat on his feet but on the outer sides, in consequence of the sole of the foot having a direction inwards, from the legs and thighs being arched outwards and the knee bent.

Nich. Pechlin, in a work written last century, entitled "*De cute Athiopum*," Albinus, and in another work, entitled "*De sede et causa coloris Athiop*," as also the great German anatomists, Meiners, Ebel, and Sœmmering, all bear witness to the fact that the muscles, blood, membranes, and all the internal organs of the body, (the bones alone excepted,) are of a darker hue in the negro than in the white man. They estimate the difference in color to be equal to that which exists between the hare and the rabbit. Who ever doubts the fact, or has none of those old and impartial authorities at hand—impartial because they were written before England adopted the policy of pressing religion and science in her service to place white American republican freemen and Guinea negroes upon the same platform—has only to look into the mouth of the first healthy typical negro he meets to be convinced of the truth, that the entire membraneous lining of the inside of the cheeks, lips and gums is of a much darker color than in the white man.

The negro, however, must be healthy and in good condition—sickness, hard usage, and chronic ailments, particularly that cachescia called consumption, speedily extracts the coloring matter out of the mucous membrances, leaving them paler and whiter than in the Caucasian.

From "God Revealed in the Process of Creation," by Prof. Jas. B. Walker.

The Specific Laws of Species.

Obedience to law is the condition upon which the safety and life of things depend. The constitution of each being is adapted to the conditions in which it was created to live. In its appropriate conditions there are provisions for its wants and sources of happiness for its enjoyment. So far as there is design in law, then, it indicates benevolence, which binds by law every thing in the condition where its happiness is procured and where its existence aids in producing the happiness of other things. Law and love are one in God. A beaver's instincts and conformations are adapted to the water; but if it should stray into the desert, where the ostrich is at home, it would meet death by protracted suffering or by the violence of other animals. The bee, by observing the laws of its life, not only secures appropriate store for itself, but, by distributing the pollen of flowers, it aids in the germination of fruits, and gives variety to the flora of the world. Thus, in obedience to the specific laws of each species, each individual not only finds happiness and life, but aids in the happiness and life of the whole. To depart from law, therefore, as necessarily secures suffering and final death, as to depart from good secures evil.

* * * * * * * *

The progress in each species is not towards another higher than itself, but to higher perfection in its own form and attributes.

www.ingramcontent.com/pod-product-compliance
Lightning Source LLC
Chambersburg PA
CBHW022148090426
42742CB00010B/1429

* 9 7 8 3 3 3 7 8 8 4 9 6 3 *